SUCCESS AMIDST DISTRESS: NEVER GIVE UP!

LA-TOYA ARTHUR-TUCKER

WORKBOOK PRESS LLC
187 E Warm Springs Rd,
Suite B285, Las Vegas, NV 89119, USA

Website: https://workbookpress.com/
Hotline: 1-888-818-4856
Email: admin@workbookpress.com

Ordering Information:
Quantity sales. Special discounts are available on quantity purchases by corporations, associations, and others.
For details, contact the publisher at the address above.

Library of Congress Control Number:
ISBN-13:   978-1-957618-04-3 (Paperback Version)
               978-1-957618-05-0 (Digital Version)

REV. DATE: 01/20/2022

Success Amidst Distress

"Never Give Up!"

Foreword

I love to read riveting, empowering and inspiring testimonies. La-Toya Arthur-Tucker captivated my mind with her life transforming experiences shared throughout *Success Amidst Distress*. This has caused me to again concur with Eleanor Roosevelt, the wife of the former American President Franklin D. Roosevelt, who postulated: *"People group through experience if they meet life honestly and courageously. This is how character is built."* This certainly epitomizes the author's route to sterling success, for many of us dream and fantasize about success, but only few actually made harden strides to truly succeed.

When navigating the changing trajectories of life, there are twists and turns, thistles and roses, and those plying its route must possess a tenacity to get to their desired destination. This writ is a true expression of the expanse that one can reach when God is allowed to be the pilot of life's journey. La-Toya Arthur-Tucker has expressed candidly and in prayerful tones, how an individual can realize his or her aspirations amidst the changing scenes of life. The pages of this book are riddled with personal testimonies of the author's rich and diverse experiences. Due to Miss Tucker's knowledge and psychological achievements, it is evident that the attitude with which these experiences were met is predicated on her Christian values and relationship with God.

What is also heart-warming is that from the author's fortifying fortress of experiences, readers will be furnished with lessons and motivational nuggets that will help charter one's course towards personal advancement. The wise man Solomon exhorts: ***"Trust in the LORD with all thine heart; and lean not unto thine own understanding. In all thy ways acknowledge him, and he shall direct thy paths"*** (Proverbs 3:5-6).

Pastor Carolyn Brandon

Director of Women, Children and Adolescents Ministries

Guyana Conference of Seventh-day Adventist.

Introduction

I was having a great morning and was excited about reaching my destination, especially since I had already missed my flight. Missing my flight was bad enough, but missing it in a strange land was worse. Thank God for kind people! I was able to get an international call, a connection was made on the island and a total stranger accommodated me for the night.

As the boat was swallowed up by the wide expanse of the Caribbean Sea, so did the feeling of loneliness engulf me. I knew no one and no one knew me. I quickly shifted my focus from the internal struggle and decided to relish the beauty of the Caribbean Sea. I was thoroughly entertained by the flying fishes, as they danced with comfort and pride. Nature provided an unexplainable relief to my distress. I was gradually engulfed with a feeling of encouragement and hope. This calm feeling was short-lived as I began to feel nauseous. This was strange, given I came from the Land of many waters and never experienced sea sickness before. I tossed a mint into my mouth but it didn't help, something was not right. I reluctantly asked the person next to me for some water, that person said they did not have, nor did the next person. Did they really not have or were they unkind people? We will see as the experience continues.

The nauseated feeling was overwhelming, so in an effort to avoid being hurt, I moved from the bench to the ground of the boat, (no worries, the boat was clean, besides I did not have time to be selective); as we would say in colloquial term, I sat on the floor. I gradually moved from the middle to the edge of the boat, holding tightly to the rail. In the distance, I heard someone saying in a Caribbean accent, *"Watch the girl moving towards the edge."* They called but I did not answer, not because I chose to ignore, but because I could not respond. I held on to the rail and the breeze kept me conscious while I vomited profusely.

At this time passengers rushed with water to my rescue. Wait a minute, these were the persons who had no water earlier, remember? I did not take the water, both hands were holding the rail, I was too weak to respond, my head stayed on the rail until I was able to see land. I lost track of time and could not give an estimated time for how long I spent in that position. What I vaguely remember was the flying fishes coming up to the side of the boat and I was somehow reassured that all will be well. The boat's horn jolted me back to reality and confirmed that I reached my destination. Despite being in distress and not knowing the outcome of my ordeal, I was reassured through nature that, all would be well!

Many people have gone through life and have never achieved their goals. So many others with big dreams and ambitions may never achieve their goals and become successful. This may not only be dependent on their choices but can also be the result of unfavourable life experiences. Regardless of your past, always remember, everything happens for a reason and a purpose that only God knows. Difficult life experiences may inspire some people to become more resilient while others become despondent. Regardless of where you are whether in pursuit of your goals and have given up on your dreams, it is never too late to make the change that puts you on the path to success. Once you have started the race, you need to keep your eyes on the finish line, have confidence in yourself and be determined. Similar to athletics, the race to your goals is not finished until you have crossed the finish line.

Table of Content

Chapter One

Humble beginnings

Being very ambitious from a tender age, I knew I wanted to be someone great, someone influential, and someone who was an exceptional leader. When asked one day by a cousin what you would like to become as an adult? I promptly responded, a Lawyer. "Hmmm", you want to tell lies" my cousin cautioned her response confused me. As a four year old I was taught not to tell lies. She further stated, "if you become a lawyer you will surely be thrown in hell fire, you cannot be a lawyer and a Christian". I immediately changed my mind from wanting to become a Lawyer to a Medical Doctor. As time progressed, I realized I had an aversion to the scent of blood. This meant I had to make a switch, I thought I should be an Accountant. No sooner had I begin to embrace my new career path, than, the resounding voices of my critics echoed out. Mercy! "From liar to thief, you need to choose something more sensible. This was implying that Lawyers are liars and Accountants are dishonest.

Some time elapsed and I gracefully embraced my teen years. This was the transformational period of my life in several ways, one accepting that I needed to start making certain decisions for myself, especially relative to my life goals and career path. Unfortunately, at this time the first two choices were definitely out, I was not in the Science stream, and was in no way poised to study law. I later learnt there were many areas of law I could have studied, but the adult dissuaded me in a very compelling way, that I didn't have second thoughts.

I was awarded a place at a high school in central Georgetown, St John's College. Life at my high school was lovely; I learnt many lessons for those five years. Lessons that have helped me to appreciate others for who they are irrespective of their ethnicity, cultural, religious or any other differences. I received racial discrimination and embarrassment, socioeconomic exclusion, among stereotypical insults. These have all motivated me to strive towards being the best I can be. During my year in fifth form, I received a great challenge that in my mind would have hampered my development, to my surprise, Jesus was just getting started to show me that He has the final say. Despite the discrimination meted out to me by one of my high school teacher, I graduated as the best graduating student in the said subject I was given some poor grades on my SBA. Here I was mistreated and unfairly graded, but when God has your future outlined, no one can change what has been written.

I completed my CXCs passing five of seven subjects and pursued sixth form. There I was thinking I was ready for a smooth sail. It was only an illusion. My challenges intensified. Not only was the competition on at the Bishops high but I felt like a stranger every day of my class. I had my own preconceived ideas about students of the Bishops high, and these did not quite help my experiences. I respected the students and not until I became an adult I completely appreciated the principles. The culture was different at the sixth form level for me in almost every aspect of my high school life. I had to eventually understand that the comparisons were not doing me well and it was not until I respected the differences for what they were that my experience was positively different. Sometimes in life we keep comparing what we have with what we had. We have to accept what we have in hand for what it is and work with the process. I eventually learnt to adapt to the new principles, many of which remained with me through my life. I recognized the need to transition from one stage to another and that has been the same process for me even after completing sixth form.

I completed high school and commenced working one week before my 18th birthday. I was excited to start earning. I was determined to achieve several things after I commenced working; one of my great plans was to work and study. After applying for a bachelor's degree at the University of Guyana, I was denied time off to complete my application process.

Understanding that my mother was depending on my income, I complied and did not complete the application process but was hoping to do it the following year. When red flags present themselves, we must be attentive. It was not very long after that disagreement with my supervisor that another disagreement was experienced. The second disagreement was greater than the first and I was completely misunderstood. I was adamant that I was in my right and even my mother recognized that I was wrongfully accused. My grandfather gave me an entire speech and at the end of all that he said he shared, "La-Toya sometimes we have to give up our rights for peace" while I did not agree with him, my mother agreed and convinced me to do what he suggested. This meant I had to apologize, it pained to apologize knowing I was not wrong, I listened and I apologized. Can you believe it after knowing I was right, agreeing to apologize to my offender and putting all my strength to do this I received this response: "I was waiting on you to come and say this, your type of people always try to stand up and express yourself knowing that you need the money and cannot do better." Those words cut me really deeply. I swallowed, listened then went straight to my desk where I typed a respectful resignation letter.

This was not expected, my supervisor tried talking to understand what happened and I was not opened to any discussion. I left I felt happy and I was pleased with my response, even though I felt like verbally expressing myself. I maintained the discipline I was taught and I was pleased about that.

I left that job not knowing where I was going to be and within one month, I received a job offer. One day I was talking to a colleague, a grown woman having overheard our conversation later called me aside and asked, have you ever considered psychology? While I did not know the meaning of the word, I was eager to understand more about the concepts, definition and general information about the word. Having done extensive research on the roles and functions of a Psychologist that was my panacea! I knew what I wanted to become and, my mind was made up. My decision was trampled upon by a number of counter opinions. "Seriously, psych what..?" "That is not an area that would make money", "only rich people do that", "You do not have the money for that area of study." One person even posited, "You want to be the kind of people who encourage spoiling children." This time, I was tenacious in my decision; I was confident that is the path I wanted to pursue. Born and raised in Georgetown, Guyana, South America, I was the first of two children for my mother and the second of five children for my father. I was by default, always part of an extended family. My maternal grandmother died when I was four (4) years old. My mother who was the eldest of seven children at the time; ages 20, 16, 14, 12, 6 and 6 months was forced take responsibility for and mother her younger siblings. Given this reality, the relationship between my aunts and uncles was more like siblings.

As I tried to grasp and comprehend my grandmother's death, tragedy struck my family once more. My stepfather, the sole breadwinner of my nine (9) members household died, a mere four (4) years after. Although I was old enough to understand the gravity of his death, the reality did not penetrate me emotionally until four (4) years after when my maternal aunt, the second of the seven siblings died.

Having experienced the death of three (3) family members in quadrennial, it seemed as though four (4) was not our lucky number. The psychological scourge of these deaths had a profound impact on my psyche. I vividly recall becoming extremely anxious with time, so much so, that I deliberately prayed for a delay of my death appointment. My plea was based on the premise that I had herculean plans and did not get to achieve my goals. The condition, I found out later were panic attacks stimulated by the thought of death. Other associated symptoms, all of which I experienced were; depression, loss of appetite, excessive worry, unexplained sadness and withdrawal. Unfortunately, my experiences went unnoticed, after all, I was just a child and my family members were too engrossed in their challenges to notice mine. This had taken a severe toll on me; it seemed like all my emotions which were bottled up had suddenly exploded. The mourning was immense because it was an amalgamation of all three deaths, my aunt, stepfather and grandmother. I was afraid of living, conscientious of the inevitable reality of death. I was terrified of going to sleep. Fortunately during this time my mother remained tenacious in her trust in God and intensified her prayer life, praying more with me and the rest of the family.

I vividly recall many times when I was too scared to share what I felt, even with my mother. I was petrified of nights and would envelop my body in the sheet as my heart raced, body shivered, and dripped with perspiration. These deaths have caused my family to survive on meager resources. At the time of my step father's death, my younger brother was seven (7) months old. My mother, who was a housewife, became the sole breadwinner of the family. She worked tirelessly to send my three aunts, my brother and I to complete school.

My mother grew in a family where domestic chores took precedence over her education; so she had only basic primary school education. However, I grew up thinking her education was high school until she explained the truth to me. Regardless, I saw my mother as intelligent, especially when she borrowed the life story of Mahatma Gandhi for me to read at age eight. I still see her as intelligent. Intelligence is not only intellectual qualities; it's the ability to apply wisdom and good judgment to decision-making.

The early childhood experiences of my mother nurtured a wealth of experiences which were reflected around the home. This augmented her skills and made her excellent at domestic jobs. She did several day jobs where she spent time cleaning for persons. Some were kind and used their consideration in remunerating her accordingly, and of course there were the unscrupulous persons who worked her to the stump and paid her meagerly.

My mother has an assertive personality; therefore, it was mental torture and much discomfort to be able to provide for us. She tolerated disrespect, and disadvantaged treatment, confident that better days were ahead. Although her earnings were little, God provided ways for us to have meals every day, regardless of how little they were, we were contented and happy as a family.

Despite her elementary education, she encouraged us daily to excel at school, and always strive to go beyond what she was able to achieve. We had to attend school every school day and every evening after we returned from school we had school work to do for mommy to grade. Even on public holidays mommy gave us school work and reading assignments.

When my mother borrowed the book I was given a two week period to complete the reading assignment. I had to tell her about what I read, moreover, she read it before me to ensure that my oral summary was accurate. I realized from early that the school routines were regular parts of my daily life so reading and spelling were my favorites. I had an aversion for math and only developed an appreciation at university.

To add to my challenges, "hand me downs" was my biggest fashion. I helped my aunts take good care of their clothes and shoes cognizant that I was next in line to receive them. At an early age I embraced some critical values imparted by my mother; not to accept things from strangers, not to be jealous of others for what they have and to be proud about what I have, regardless of how little it was. As the song writer truthfully expressed, "little is much when God is in it", I can attest; to seeing food multiply to meet the needs of my entire family, time and time again. Indeed, God be praised!

Regardless of the beginning of one's life, when Jesus gets in the midst the outcome always changes. Individuals may have a rough start or several forms of setbacks, it is important to remember that yesterday was a "cancelled cheque, tomorrow is a promissory note and today is definitely cash in hand". As the famous proverb states "make hay while the sunshine". To all my readers, many of the most famous and successful people in the world evolved humble beginnings and so can you!

Daydreaming was a regular practice of mine, as I grew older I learnt, not only did I daydream, I envisioned where I wanted to be and set realistic goals. There is nothing too great for God to handle, always remember, Philippians 4:13, "I can do ALL things through Christ who strengthens me", this text has a wealth of power that can activate your courage and inner strength, if you only believe that you can achieve and receive the success God has in store for you.

Lesson Learnt

Regardless of your starting point in life, the race has to begin. Your pace, attitude and altitude will definitely determine the time of completion, and overall achievement in the race.

Motivational Tip

You were destined for greatness. The sooner you start your journey to the destination of greatness the earlier you will reach there.

Chapter Two
"Unrecognized Treasures"

The thought of being unrecognized is unpleasant. The onset of COVID 19 has brought many things to the forefront. Many discoveries were made within the home. Things went unnoticed and it took a pandemic to reveal many things, persons, places and ideas to the knowledge of others. Society has a way of recognizing that which is already known.

The primary school I attended was not recognized by many within the community. Many parents transferred their children to other schools. My mother decided that I will and should stay at the school as she believed "everything happens for a reason that only God knows." This has always been her mantra and she has trained us to respect divine outcomes.

St Sidwell's Primary when it was functional, was located at Hadfield and Vlissengen Road, situated on the southern side of the 1763 monument in Georgetown, Guyana. The building still exists but the school is not operational, at least not as it was when I attended. This school was not even known by many Guyanese living in Georgetown. I still have to describe my primary school to persons, as recent as 2021.

As unpopular and non-recognized as the school was, I had to attend, and I happily told persons the name of my school when they asked, even when their facial expressions dampened my enthusiasm. Our inner joys should remain jubilant despite what others think. Persons will always have negatives to share. If we allow the views, opinions and perspectives of others to constantly determine what we do, there may be situations of not many things being done.

While it is good to take counsels from others, listen to the different perspectives, views and opinions; there should be a healthy balance and we should use our experiences to teach us how much of what others express we should accept and more so allow to guide and influence out actions and decisions.

With my school being a low performing institution, the students were labelled. Self-Fulfilling prophecies were made against many students. This was rather unfortunate. Some students were only trying to become the brightest star. It is unbelievable how many persons were forced and are still being forced off the path of success by others, more so others who have greater hope of achieving their success.

Many individuals believe success should only be written in specific communities, families and institutions. Each of us has greatness deep within. Stop, take a deep breath and read that line one more time, just in case you missed it, remember, each of us has greatness deep within. Our goals may be similar but we must understand that we can be geniuses in different areas. Every person's success does not have to be the same. The more we collaborate and assist each other, the more successful society we will have and ultimately a better space with which we can interact, but then again, we wonder how can this be, it is simple, the change must start within, hence the change must start with me, yes you am talking to.

My challenges intensified as I prepared for Common Entrance, (now called National Grade Six Examination). I started attending a lesson at another school and things were going better. As time progressed and got closer to the exam date, I had to stop attending the extra classes, since the Teacher started teaching only students from her school.

While everyone had all their text books, I had only some that mommy borrowed from a friend. I used them carefully and wisely since they were not mine. My primary school then started giving extra classes at school on Saturdays, I refused to attend and my mother supported my decision 100%. This was my first official trial that I can remember after giving my life to Jesus in 1995.

Having been baptized as a member of the Seventh-day Adventist Church, Saturday, the Seventh-day of the week is the Lord's Sabbath. As young as I was, I respected the Sabbath and I still do. I was also concerned about what was going to be done since nothing much was done during the 5 days school week.

All of my friends were able to attend lessons at various schools and centers. However, my mother could not afford the fees, so I had to work with the little resources I had at the time, I worked with the help of my older aunts and mother every weekday evening and on Sundays. I did the exam and results revealed that I came third at Sidwell's Primary in 1996; I scored marks for St. John's College in Georgetown as well. This was awesome news for me. My mother was very proud. She bought me a gift, took me out for a treat and she verbally expressed joy.

Many individuals saw my potentials and instead of encouraging me, they said negative things to try to keep me down. One woman called me one day, and asked why I was not going to extra classes during the holidays. Before I could even respond she commented, "Bright, bright children going extra classes and you not going and expect to pass." Even though I was still young, I knew what she was trying to say, with the teachings my mother gave me, I knew I had to be respectful to my elders so I smiled and went on, of course my answer would not have made a difference, since she had already made a conclusion. Not only did she consider me a "dunce", but she also told me I was going to fail. Her remarks were packed with so many negatives. I have always strived to keep a positive outlook on thinks. This propelled me to keep my focus.

I often thought, will you ever attain success? While I am not insane, I answered the question whenever it was asked in my head with a resounding YES! My idea of success is not the attainment of assets and material things, while that is great to achieve. I recognized from early that I had a strong desire to be the best I can be. This was certainly an unrecognized treasure. As I grew older, I learnt it was my intrinsic motivation. I have a strong intrinsic motivation to excel and do excellently at any activity or task I set out to achieve or complete.

My idea of success is being able to reach my goals and achieve my purpose in life. Being able to remain humble and reaching others, helping them to reach their goals. Nothing is wrong with achieving assets and material things, something is wrong if we trample on others to get them, something is even bothersome, if we strive to achieve them at all cost, including harming, hurting or damaging others. Will you strive to reach yours success? What method will you take to reach your success? Yes, you can and you should strive to achieve your success! You need to believe that you can and indeed you will receive and achieve your success.

Lesson Learnt

There are some decisions that are better made, when we make the choice for ourselves. We must accept responsibility for our actions. We must recognize our hidden passions, abilities and dreams. We must choose to make healthy decisions.

Motivation Tip

Every day we make decisions. Choose today to be the day that you will make a decision that you will never forget, make that decision to stick with your plan to achieve success despite the distress you experience. Keeping your focus, and you will strengthen your internal locus.

Chapter Three

"Stumbling blocks to stepping stones"

I undoubtedly thought I had achieved something worthy, but was oblivious to the fact that St. John's College was seen as a school which was stereotyped as "below acceptable standard". My mother, however, did not share those sentiments, as she was extremely proud of my achievement and so were my other family members, relatives and friends. During my five years of secondary school, there were good times as well as challenges. As I reminisce on the relics of the past, most of those good times were the time spent with friends, especially Michelle and Tonya.

It was discouraging to attend a school that is categorized as "Low grade" by Society. However, as I increased in wisdom and understanding, I came to accept that your school doesn't determine your future, rather it's the goals you set and dream you have for yourself that serves more as a determinant of your future. My early childhood school was almost invisible, known only by the persons who attended it. I recall having a friend from kindergarten, nursery school as we say in Guyana; oh how I enjoyed spending time with her. We were very good friends and were coincidentally placed at the same Primary school. No sooner had she started her new school, then her mother decided to transfer her to what was considered "one of the top Primary schools" in Georgetown. I later discovered that my friend was placed back one class lower. Nevertheless, I eventually overcame the hurt of parting with my friend and moved on. For a while, we greeted each other whenever we connected on the streets, but the exuberance of seeing each other eventually faded with time. I embraced the new school term with dignity and pride, having been promoted now to Grade 8, I was eager to meet the new students entering the school. As I scanned the room of nervous and curious students, my gaze came upon a familiar feature. I stood for a while in disbelief, surprised and curious, I was finally reunited with my long lost friend, unfortunately however, she was in one grade lower. To my surprise there I was standing one grade higher than my long lost friend. We were nevertheless, excited to see each other. Wait! Reality hit me, my friend who was transferred to a more renowned Primary school passed her Common Entrance Examination for the same high school as me, nothing was wrong with my friend, nor her school. Something was wrong with the perspective of some members of society and how they marginalize others for no reason. She was transferred because the primary school was seen as a non-performing school. This is a candid lesson that it does not matter what school you attend, but rather your willingness to achieve and the attitude you bring as an individual.

I received prizes for academic performance each year, amidst the limited resources that were available to me. One school term in my first year of secondary school, I scored 0% on a class test, the teacher obviously knowing my potential expressed disappointment openly. I was embarrassed, my classmates mocked me openly.

This motivated me to rid all attitudes of complacency and to strive towards achieving the highest. That same school term I ensured that I studied more than ever before; at the end of the following school term I scored 100% on the very test I previously scored 0%. This showed me that success can be achieved by all, if we are determined. That was my launching pad and from that term onward I ensured that

I worked assiduously to move from one class to the next. This inspired me to believe that I should always excel and not study just to pass, but rather to score grades at exceptional levels. Accepting average, limits anyone's potential, hence as intelligent beings we should strive to achieve our highest goals, dreams and aspirations.

I was discriminated against in many instances during high school, especially because of my stature. In addition to being considered short by others, my ethnicity and socio-economic status were all sources of discrimination. It was interesting to experience how humanity considered themselves. People who elevate themselves better than others, often mistreat others. Let me share a wise council, to those who have discriminated against me and others. If the short persons were not around you would not have known that you were tall. To the rich, it's the poor that makes you know that you're rich. Instead of segregating ourselves from others because of our differences we should appreciate and embrace our differences. If everyone were the same, darn! This earth would have been so boring. Thank God for variety and diversity. Despite the many acts of discrimination meted against me, I was always encouraged by my family especially my mother to aim for the stars.

As time progressed, my years at St. John's College showed and taught me some valuable life lessons. My mother could not have afforded to provide us with lunch money, so she baked and cooked our snacks. All our snacks and lunches were baked. Every day during break and lunch time came, I would watch with longing, as the children rushed to the canteen. I would sometimes happily eat what my mother had prepared.

There were times when I was unhappy, especially when the

food provided by my mother was not something I liked. To this day I dislike "conkies" also known as "Tie leaf" or "blue draws". It is an African dish containing cornmeal, coconut, raisins or sweet potato. I remembered taking that to school more than once in one week. My mother was only ensuring that we had something to eat.

I recognized one afternoon that the canteen operators collected used drink bottles and refunded $10.00 and $20.00. I shouted hooray! This became my new little business venture, I collected bottles and returned them after school to the canteen and accumulated some much needed spending money. Many of the students found it a pleasure giving me their empty drink bottles to return to the canteen. They were ignorant of the rewards I received for returning the bottles to the canteen. In their minds they were using me as their helper.

I was delighted to serve as their helper, for my benefits were tangible. My small consistent earnings helped to buffer some of my daily expenses. I was able to pay my own bus fare and take care of some other little needs. There were some times when I had the impression that my peers were deliberately taking advantage of me, as they relished the sight of me constantly relieving them of their used drink bottles. While they saw me granting them small favors, I knew the far reaching impact of this seemingly frivolous activity.

The secret was out! My peers eventually found out what was happening and as you guessed, stopped giving me their bottles. This action brought discomfort and sadness. Additionally, they were upset, not necessarily about the bottles but that the canteen was giving money in exchange. They wanted me to return the bottles for FREE! I was taught to work hard for whatever I wanted so I saw my efforts of taking the bottles back to the canteen as a form of work.

The students who started returning their own bottles eventually became complacent and eventually stopped. Once again the bottles remained in the classroom and my business which was on pause, resumed. This taught me a valuable lesson. Sometimes we see people doing things without knowing their reason and try to outcompete and take opportunities away from them. However, when a person has a goal, they will withstand the challenges and continue to pursue it. The competitors will soon be dissuaded if that's not their goal. Hence, I resumed my bottle trade and continued to reap the benefits. These challenges though experienced young have strengthened my fortitude and propelled me towards my goals. This was an awakening moment for me as I became aware that there will always be individuals who can't fathom your dreams and will serve as obstacles to the process. However, instead of seeing them as obstacles, they were my motivators to keep pressing forward. Moreover, they served as my intrinsic motivator. I am determined to finish the race I have started. Those experiences reminded me of my journey, the relics of my past and aspiration of the future I was determined to create, indeed, I can reach my success.

One day I received an assignment that seemed very complicated and had to utilize the services at the National Library. My efforts, however, proved futile. I subsequently informed my subject teacher and he advised me on which book I should use. The National Library hadn't the book, so I asked one of my classmates to Borrow her own during the regular school hours. I happily received it and completed my assignment. To my satisfaction, I scored the highest on the assignment 9/10 out of a class of 30 students, the second place student scored 3/10, which was an indication that the scores of the other students were definitely below 3/10. The subject teacher expressed disappointment in the Class' performance and commended me for a job well done. At this time, I became the center of attention. My classmate who lent me the book, boldly asked: "which book did you use La-Toya?" The class teacher was still standing before the class, as silence pierced the room and all attention shifted to me. "Well, I used your book that I borrowed." "My book? "I am never lending my books to another **black person,** I should have listened to my mother", my classmate blurted out in anger. Honestly, I was embarrassed and at the same time, proud of my performance and my ethnicity that was being ridiculed. The silence was deafening for a few minutes, but I thought to myself, "thank God for His goodness." This was my first encounter with ethnic discrimination, however, I learnt my lesson. I never asked the girl to borrow another book, but God saw me through.

My secondary school journey was coming to an end. I was now in fourth form (grade 10). While seeking permission from businesses to do my School-based Assessment (SBA), for Principles of Business, I received many negative responses from businesses. One business operator told me, they do not give out their information for SBAs, I respected their response and continued my search. To my surprise, when our SBAs were all completed and we were showing our SBAs to each other, I was shocked to see a student of a different ethnicity with the same business that told me they do not give their information for SBAs. After a brief and subtle conversation, I realized that I have received ethnic discrimination for the second time.

These experiences motivated me to strive to be different. One day while going to school, a grown man stopped me and said, "good morning, you are an intelligent young lady, you can reach very far in life, if you only persevere and reach your goals." I did not know this man apart from seeing him sometimes while I traversed the streets to school. His words of encouragement further boosted my confidence, I smiled and thanked him for his encouragement. He further lamented that if he had the opportunities and knowledge that I have, he would have been a different individual. Many individuals do not appreciate what they have until they would have lost it. I urge you to accept whatever little resources you have and use it to the best of your ability to reach for your success.

I was very active in high school; I participated in athletics, cricket, volleyball and circle tennis. I was a part of the bible club, quiz competition, and even danced at school concerts. Basically, I was in every club or activity except the choir, as you may have guessed, singing wasn't my gift. I enjoyed high school years despite the varied and many challenges. I saw them as stepping stones and motivators. I had friends from different grades, ethnicities and sizes. I love variety. To my teachers, I was a saint but I did do some unsavory things. I graduated from St. John's College with 5 passes at the Caribbean Examination Council (CXC), after which I gained acceptance at the Bishops" High school, lower sixth to do CAPE; where I did 3 Cape subjects, Communications Studies, Caribbean Studies and Sociology. I successfully passed all three of my CAPE subjects.

Life at the Bishops' High was not the same as it was at St. John's College. The cultures within the two schools were different. I was the only person from St. John's College that went to lower sixth at The Bishops' high in 2001. I spent seven months at Bishops'. These short months, seemed like seven years to me. They were intense, Bishops' was a Senior Secondary School with extremely high standards. I have learnt many valuable lessons and learnt to adapt to the environment; the additional rules, teaching methods and even the students.

I was familiar with attending schools that were unknown. This time around I attended a known school, but was still seen by many for where I came from and who and where I was. Persons believed I did not deserve being at the school. Can you believe that? As humans we are so judgmental, mean and unkind to each other.

I vividly recall after CXC, a grown woman enquired about my performance? When I shared it with her she was shocked and posited "it could have been worse though, so what are you going to do now?" I expressed interest in going to continue my education and she sought to dissuade me. In exasperation, she later transferred her child from the school, as she stated "her child is too intelligent to be in the same class with me". I smiled in compassion for her level of reasoning. I am happy intelligence is not something we can count like we can count money or Oreos in a packet.

Moving confidently into my new chapter, I signed up to do three (3) subjects at Cape. Once again my demotivators tried to influence my decision by assuming I couldn't handle three (3) subjects and should do less. The Head teacher of the school advised students to do how many subjects they can manage. With confidence, I knew had the aptitude and propensity to succeed, I persisted with my three (3) subjects. As I reflect it is evident that my Head teacher was a true educator. It is never a good thing to "box students in". I do understand that sometimes teachers think they can accurately evaluate Students' potential, but there are many instances where they misjudge students' abilities. To my chagrin, one relative said to me, "I think you should drop a subject, students who gained distinctions at CXC have failed, so why should you do all three? Given my resilient personality, I listened to all the advice but remained tenacious in my position to write three subjects.

I did not do History or Geography at CXC level, so I paid more attention in Caribbean studies than any other subject. One day I made an appointment to see my subject teacher for Caribbean Studies, when I arrived at the staff room, I was told she was not there. I checked back a little while later and I was told the same thing. I stood outside the staff room to wait until she returned. To my surprise, she was in the staff room. I humbly asked another teacher to call her she eventually came and to my disappointment commented that she remembered my appointment, but she was too busy to attend to me. During my discussion with her, she paused to say; "I am impressed at your perseverance, if you continue with this attitude, you will achieve your goals." Many individuals did not know that this was my weakest subject at lower sixth, because when I was in class, I echoed all the answers that the students were afraid to say; 98% of the time I was correct. Sometimes the teacher called on me to answer questions, I used my background knowledge and what I read outside of class time to answer the questions. I intensified my reading and research to be on par in class.

The day of validation finally came, I my first Cape exam. I almost fainted seeing one question worth 50 points. I thanked God that I was able to successfully complete the examination for all three subjects. The wait for the results was filled with anxiety. When the day finally came and I arrived at school to collect my cape results, my heart pounded and my hands were wet from nervousness. Although the negative utterances which have bombarded my goal remained etched in my memory, I confidently moved towards the Principal's Office to uplift my results. After what seemed like eternity, my mind was jolted back to reality by my Principal's comments, "Congratulations Ms. Arthur, you have successfully passed all three of your subjects." Full of elation, I couldn't wait to get home to give my mother the remarkable news. Her screams could have shattered my eardrum, "God be praised!"

I left sixth form in 2002, uncertain of my next move. I stayed at home for eleven (11) months. During these months, I did basic computer classes to keep my brain occupied. It is my firm belief that time should not be wasted. Those months were not the brightest; the computer classes were not sufficient to occupy my time, move over, I sent several applications out seeking jobs and received all negative responses. A breakthrough finally came when I received my first job in March 2003.

The experience of waiting taught me many valuable lessons. However, the most pertinent one was to wait on the Lord. Other lessons learnt were: in life you would not always get what you want; and it is important to remember that we must work hard at whatever juncture we are until we get to where and what we want. I used my first job as a launching pad to garner relevant work experience. Although being a Clerical staff was not my type of job, I did my best in every task I had. Conflicts came, some I accepted and acknowledged my error and others where I knew I was right but gave up that right for peace. Further, I recalled a specific situation where I accepted fault and I apologized only because my mother advised me to. To my annoyance, the recipient of the apology ecstatic, saying "I had to apologize, and it was only persons of a certain socio-economic group do what I did then have to apologize". This was a job whereby I was convinced that I was given tasks that were not within my job description. While I had no problem executing them because I saw them as learning experiences, I was not compensated. When I enquired about my services being abused, I was described as rude and confrontational.

As I reflected on the dilemma, there were other young individuals at my work place who endured similar plights. Anticipating that my situation would eventually spiral out of control, it was time to make a decision and I had to do so quickly. I requested time-off to attend an orientation at the University of Guyana, where I applied to study and I was boldly told, "I will not be granting you this time off because you want to qualify yourself to leave my job". Since my manager was so bold at sharing her thoughts that I considered selfish, wicked and vindictive, I decided I will not be selfish about expressing my intentions.

I did not express them to her but I did to my family. My mother kept encouraging me to be respectful, which I always ensured I did. However, on the day of the incident mentioned above, I was very close to my breaking point. I was called derogatory names and it was unbearable, I left the office and yes, I slammed a door. I was further reprimanded verbally for slamming the door. Unfortunately, during the entire ordeal, I was not given the opportunity to speak. Consequently, I was described as rude, insubordinate and disrespectful. My mother again encouraged me to keep calm and apologize. After all of this I offered an apology but the unsavory treatment worsened. I had reached my breaking point and this time penned an interesting letter of resignation.

Unemployed and broken, I recommenced my job hunting. An important paradox in this narrative is that I did not resign because of our disagreement but rather because it was explicit that my former employer was deliberate in not supporting my goals of advancing my education. She was also partial, discriminative and comfortable stigmatizing me.

This experience helped me to validate the notion that trials are thrown at us definitely to make us stronger. I went on to complete my BSc. in Psychology amidst much apprehension and discouragement from persons around me, that this field of study was not in demand and I would not be gainfully employed. Nevertheless, trials help to refine us, and make us glitter after we successfully come through them. Trials are like the refiners' fire, the heat is strong but the result is great. There are times when the heat is up and we feel trapped, these are the times that determine our strength. These are the times our trust and loyalty to God should be exhibited from every end. We are more than conquerors through Jesus Christ (Romans 8:37). Without Him where would we have been? I don't know, but one thing I do know that God's love is true.

My friends there will be times in life where situations are upon you, and you will have to humble yourself and stoop to conquer. It is important to remember that we should not compromise our morals, principles and goals to suit anyone. Neither undermine our respect and Christian values to accommodate anyone. God has done it in times past for many men and my life is testimony that He can do the very same for you and all who trust him.

We all can attain success if we allow King Jesus to help us climb our mountains and walk the seemingly rough road on our journey to success. The situation may be depressing, you may be perplexed or discouraged, but there is always that hope that can truly help us if we only believe.

Lesson Learnt

*Not every embarrassing situation is meant
to put you to shame. Always wear a smile
instead of a frown. Your humility through
embarrassment may be all it takes to
illustrate lifelong lesson to an onlooker*

Motivational Tip

*You may stumble, you may tumble or
even fumble, but never let anyone see
or make you crumble.*

"Success is a Continuous Journey"

By: La-Toya Arthur-Tucker

Discouragement, feeling battered and worn

Why does it have to happen to me?

In moments like these my thoughts seem torn

I cry, reflect and keep fighting to be the best I can be
Then I remember it is all a part of my journey.

The journey to success can sometimes feel difficult

I struggle to keep up and often stumble

Amidst tears, distress, frustration and tumult

My dream of success would never crumble

Hurdles come from here, there and everywhere

My passion for achievement will always stay

This I must remember is all a part of my journey.

When I feel tempted to give up

Even when I am tempted to let go and keep silent

My intrinsic motivation helps me to be resilient

Oh yes I am reminded it is a journey

One that is continuous and as such I will be
victorious.

Chapter Four

"Disappointments can be blessings too"

The completion of my BSc. with honors propelled me to complete my Master's degree. However, with each accomplishment I became thirsty for more knowledge; I was determined to pursue doctoral studies. With great passion and enthusiasm, applications were sent out. I received positive responses from every institution. However, I had no financial support. Nevertheless, I was not going to be deterred from my quest for my success. I eventually was able to find an institution where I had the option to work and study. Strangely enough, I had applied and received the job, everything was done virtually even years before the pandemic. I was expected in that country within two months" following my acceptance, to commence my new job. The situation looked promising, except that I had my final interview pending. I had already received my scores for exams done, and my records were in order.

The day came for me to do my interview and at that time I had a one year old toddler who caused major disturbances to that process. There was no one around to assist with baby sitting and my husband had to work. The moment I hoped for had arrived; the email was seen in my inbox from the university. I was excited and nervous simultaneously as I clicked and opened the mail which read in a brief synopsis:

"Dear La-Toya having reviewed your profile, it was voted that acceptance be denied" I was unable to read the rest of the content; my heart sank to a dark place. I recalled the exact moment when a questioned was asked and I answered while trying to keep little Jenae focused and I answered incorrectly. I eventually corrected my response, but my responses were distracted. I felt depressed, disappointed and it seemed like I had failed totally.

I reflected about the experience for days, not only was I distracted during the interview but was embarrassed as little daughter Jenae continuously pressed on and off the camera. I kept replaying everything in my head, asking questions and answering them as well. What exactly happened on that day? As panic and frustration engulfed me, I answered questions I knew incorrectly and the entire interview was just a mess. As I read the letter almost every day, I remembered seeing a part of the email that stated: you can reapply whenever you are ready. I was plunged into depression as my goal was to complete my third degree by age 35. I had everything in place, and on that day my dreams collapsed. I blamed my husband for going to work and was upset with our little angel for ruining my opportunity; I was just bitter. In the weeks ahead, I reflected on the situation and I recognized I was being too hard on myself and on my family. I was now ashamed. This introspection brought to the fore my unpreparedness mentally and emotionally for doctoral studies.

My greatest disappointment was the fact that I was not accepted. More often than not, we are oblivious to how to deal with rejection... After some weeks of feeling despondent, I accepted the reality; I needed to turn the flash light within and use the experience to be better at being me. I therefore started diverting my energy to being a better wife, a better mother and a better person.

I understood if I had gone to study at that time, our daughter would have been deprived of her motherly affections and attention. My husband definitely would have been deprived of my presence and attention as well. I thought long and hard, was it what I really wanted? I was being selfish, I was only thinking about me. All I was seeing was me and my goals. I was not taking the needs of my family into consideration.

When the revelation came to me about how selfish I was I had to humble myself and apologize to my family. I invested more energy in family time. After doing this I started feeling better. I started regaining my joys and my momentum.

Sometimes we strive to achieve our goals at the detriment of our family and friends. It is not good and we should **NEVER** do this. What sense will it make to achieve great things, with no one to join in celebration? When our achievements receive support from those closest to us, we feel more fulfilled. I shelved the thought of furthering my studies and focused on being a stay at home mother, where I concentrated my efforts on home schooling our daughter. ***sighs*** it seemed like I am ever putting myself into the spotlight for public opinion. The demeaning comments and questions started coming, "home schooling", "can you even afford that?" One person told me I should put my education to use within a place of employment and not within my home.

We discussed and planned and decided to extend our family. This was successfully completed with the addition of our son. I was determined to ensure that I contributed towards the foundation of our children's education. This helped my husband and I to agree, that our children were not going to be in any day care settings. Nothing is wrong with day cares; we just decided that we did not want that for our children.

Despite the many negative perceptions evoked by our decisions, they motivated us and served as fuel to our flames. On the contrary, there were persons who continuously prayed for us and showed us love. Those persons gave us hope in humanity and provided reassurance that everything will work out fine. We relished those edifying interactions.

Always Believe in yourself. Reminiscing on my journey, the possibility of completing my Doctorate Degree before age 40, looked impossible. I am currently enrolled in an international University completing my second year of doctoral studies. Guess what? Not only am I studying, I have been granted a scholarship! Truth be told, while I was still completing my undergraduate degree I said it casually, "I would like to complete my three degrees by age 35". I said it with no conviction. Although I persisted, I did not have the confidence, which I now exhibit embracing the power of a dream.

After I was rejected from the university as shared in chapter 3, I have grown to accept that I was not yet ready, although that conviction came after. Having realized that things can happen when we believe,

I started setting astronomical goals which seem impossible in my current construct than it seemed in my imagination.

Reflecting on the relics of my childhood, I imagined having experience with persons of different cultures, with different accents and experiences different from mine. At the time when I had that imagination, I had never even travelled before. I travelled for the first time at the age of 15. However, years later, my imagination, will-power, and determination, did not only see me attending an international university, but I married into a foreign culture, where I am forever hearing a different accent.

I am a Guyanese to the bone, and that will always be! However, that doesn't undermine my many international friends, especially Jamaicans and I love them dearly. I love them equally, as I love my own nationals.

I finally completed my first book and was extremely excited to actually have landed within the world of authorship. However, the brilliant flame was smothered shortly after it ignited because to date, I have not officially launched my first book. It seemed like success for me remains elusive. That thought, I constantly dismiss and challenge as erroneous and is adamant it will not envelop mental faculty nor cloud my vision.

It is interesting to see how our lives can unfold such great blessings and our dreams can be revealed in the appropriate time.

Therefore, whatever goal you aspire to achieve, with the right attitude, dedication, determination, and support you can achieve it! You need to pray about it, if you are not a spiritual person and do not believe in prayers, with the right attitude you can be led to achieving equally. Take time to dream, meditate and keep a focused attitude.

Lesson Learnt

Whatever your mind conceive, when you believe you can achieve, never give up on your dreams

Motivational Tip

Many successful folks have started their journey through simply using their imagination. Do not erase your imagination, put it in writing or in drawing, with the determination what it moves form a mere thought, to three D, then reality

Chapter Five

"Changes bring Challenges"

*L*ike many girls, I had fantasies of my wedding day, the decor, my dress, food, ceremony among many other feminine things, it's the one time in your life you want everything to be perfect. That imagination, however, certainly didn't cater for my unexpected encounter. The beautiful invitations were printed and distributed. My then boyfriend and I did a photo shoot for the invitations. The invitations were expressive and recipients did not hide their commendations in that regard. The time was winding down. We travelled to our wedding destination and were busy completing some transactions and preparations. The reception hall was already booked. We were at the seamstress to do some minor adjustments to the Bridesmaids' dresses, just to confirm that everything was in shape. The food and drinks were ordered, the venue set to be decorated and all the arrangements made to execute the wedding. Moreover, international guests made the sacrifice and investment to share the special moment with us. My wedding was abruptly postponed two days prior to the scheduled date of the wedding. Yes! You have read right! A mere two days before that big day, as you would have guessed, all systems were in place by then.

This was how everything started to collapse, my phone rang and from the sound of the caller I sensed something was wrong. The person was screaming in a sorrowful manner which made me petrified. My fiancé saw the look on my face and drew closer. Not only was the person in tears but the news the person gave paralyzed me physically, mentally and emotionally for a few minutes. After being jolted back to reality, we hurriedly left the location where we were and on our way home made arrangements for an urgent family meeting. This was a difficult decision to make and we couldn't do it alone. Most of the guests were already in the country, others were making preparation to get to our location. The meat was already prepared, cake baked and everything had to be placed on an abrupt pause. Thankfully the support was there from our family. After examining all the extenuating circumstances, the decision was made to postpone the wedding. The entire family present immediately sprang into action and news was communicated to the rest of the family and potential guests. A family member who was integrally involved in the wedding had a crisis and this created a ripple effect. We were all affected by this crisis and our wedding had to be rescheduled. Emotions flared in our meeting and people expressed their disappointment, thoughts and feelings aggressively. I was then forced to intervene and utilize my conflict resolution skills. Tempers flared, interpersonal differences collided and what started out distasteful was steered to an amicable resolution.

My fiancé and I took some time away from everyone, where we reflected, supported each other and decided on the way forward. This decision was shared with our families who agreed and finally, a beam of hope began to emerge. Four months after the ordeal, we were walking down the aisle.

It was a bitter-sweet moment because some of our guests were unable to return, however, there were others who were unable to travel in August 2012 but made it for December. On January 1, 2013, we were officially married and there has never been any regrets except we felt we should have been married much earlier, however, this would not have been possible in light of our varied priorities.

This was a rough start to our union; we desired to last for eternity. However, it was a valuable life lesson that on the road to achieving our goals, we may sometimes have to detour, pause or remove obstacles. In 2021, my husband and I celebrated eight (8) years of marriage and we love every moment of the experience. I asked my husband the question; if you had to choose a wife again who would you choose? He eagerly answered, I would choose my La-Toya again and again, and I certainly would do the same, choose my Junior Tucker. Whatever is meant to be, will always be. The union has blossomed and bore two beautiful fruits.

The experience has taught us many important lessons. What seems like a disappointment could actually be an appointment. It depends on how we look at things. Family, members should be supportive of each other. Communication is always a key element of our interpersonal interactions; it should be done objectively. When we allow our emotions to guide us and dominate our expressions, we are likely to say and do things that may have lasting implications. We must ensure that whatever we choose to do is done from a genuine and responsible place in our hearts.

Many people were upset with the decision that we made. In life people will always be upset with our choices, but we must make the choice that is aligned with our goals. What started out lovely, seemed like a disappointment, and just when we thought we met a road block, it was a diversion to another leg of the journey.

Family Expansion

When we got married, I was in the final year of my graduate studies. My husband was in graduate school as well. We both had academic demands. It was challenging in some regards but fun in others, especially when we challenged each other within the classroom. We both knew what we wanted from each other and this made things so much easier.

We quickly accepted that we were not as young as we thought, or I should probably say as young as we looked. We accepted our reality although after we married we were still referred to by strangers when they saw us in public as 'little'.

We enjoyed that title but couldn't ignore our reality, we were aging and needed to make decisions, not as boyfriend and girlfriend but as husband and wife.

We were both afraid of the new roles but we were confident that we would make the discoveries and cross hurdles together. We were ready as a team to conquer the obstacles before us, after all, we were able to conquer what seemed like an impasse before we said "I do."

I started sleeping rather excessively. Understanding that we were studying, we figured I needed some well-deserved rest after doing some late night assignments and preparation for exams. The sleeping became more pronounced as I was falling asleep in class. My Professors observed the change and reminded me that I need to rest better at night to avoid sleeping in classes.

While I was trying to manage my sleeping habits, there was something else that greeted me. Upon visiting the school's cafeteria I noticed I became nauseous. While sharing this with my husband, I had to rush to the bathroom. Not only was I nauseous at school, but while hubby cooked, I could not manage the smell. This was rather strange. All the time this was happening, though it happened in quick succession, no one thought of seeking medical help.

Having kept a consistent documentation of my monthly appointments with Mother Nature, I noticed she did not fulfil her monthly visit with me. So I thought this was strange, I immediately purchased a pregnancy test. I was calm before the purchase. However, excitement built up at the Pharmacy and I could not manage to look at the test results after it was done. My husband and I were excited with the news; we were expecting our first child. Actually, he was more excited than me, I was scared.

I didn't have any of my relatives or family members with me. It was only my husband and I. With my dear friend, Tashika's encouragement and support, my courage was restored. My other close friends also supported in every way possible through the different means technology afforded them to be of help to me.

This was a journey of a lifetime. Not only was I nervous but also experienced some of the worst pregnancy related symptoms. Despite being hospitalized for three nights and two days, it was still a beautiful experience. This was my first encounter being hospitalized. I was worried, but with several motivators and motivational experiences, I was still clinging to my thread of hope.

My husband sat with the doctor as they explored options. My medication was changed several times and none seemed to work that is when the doctor related to my husband that he has no other choice than to admit me. My husband pleaded with the doctor, but the doctor had to make a decision in my best interest.

The nurses had to attend to me while they gathered information from my husband. He did an excellent job in gathering my stuff from home and returning quickly. By the next morning, a team of doctors and nurses were around me and I was informed that I was diagnosed with **Hyperemesis gravidarum.** I searched for it on Google to understand what it was. It was an extreme form of morning sickness. I lost a significant amount of weight and my diet was restricted to specific sets of food. Many people told me it was all a part of the pregnancy journey, but it was all new to me and I had to find ways of coping. There were many times when my mental health was not where it was supposed to be, I became depressed, stressed, anxious, confused, sad and the list went on. Many times, my husband bore the brunt of it all. He understood that it was a difficult time for both of us. He was constantly supportive and always strived to ensure that I had all that I needed.

First trimester came and ended, and the second trimester was much better. It became better after the halfway mark of that trimester approached.

Heading into the third trimester brought some uncertainties but I prayed more and insisted on working more with my husband. It was an awesome experience to have listened to Jenae's heartbeat, watch her movement through the skin of my tummy, or through my clothes and even participate in activities with her while she was in the womb.

I remembered one evening my dearly beloved husband thought Jenae was too exposed to psychology, so he felt she needed more exposure to music. He connected the music boxes to his keyboard and they had song service. That Sabbath evening, we sang and he played while he sang and we had a wonderful worship experience. Jenae danced happily in the womb. I eventually went to sleep while my husband continued to serenade our unborn much to her delight... These activities were punctuated when I changed position and requested the music be stopped and lights touted. A mere ten minutes later, she was quiet and I returned to sleep.

My experiences during pregnancy proved that training of children begins from within the womb.

The day came and I received my cue that it was time to give birth. I walked very piously into the hospital. Walked up the stairs and calmly communicated to the nurse that I was in labour. To my surprise, I was rudely asked, "What makes you think you are ready?" I pleasantly responded, I am experiencing all the symptoms of labour. The Nurse took a step back then asked me to sit. There are times when we have indicators to guide our course of action and people who are oblivious to that will try to determine our course. Instead we should remain focused and consistently alert.

I was admitted and the rest of my journey was a pleasant one, no pain, except for an abrasive doctor who was physically rough, I tried my best to keep calm, stayed happy and motivated for a successful delivery, eagerly awaiting my daughter. I slept through the night peacefully... However, the next morning, raised some anxiety as my bedside attracted a team of doctors. I overheard a doctor saying, "but this cannot be", he came and asked me my age, then he returned to the team. They were very attentive and whatever they were discussing seemed important. I was curious to know what they were discussing; I tried to listen butt… I could not hear clearly. Based on my height and size according to the doctor, my tummy was too big. I did not bother to ask for an explanation, although I was very inquisitive. I was taken to a separate room where further examination was done on my abdomen and other parts of my body. The doctor nicely informed me of the procedure that they have to do. He asked me to "remain still for the next half of an hour". In his exact words, please go and remain on your bed. He told me I will feel intense pain and it will get sharper and shaper after 30 minutes. It seemed like the doctor's clock went through the window, before I returned to the bed, in less than five minutes pain was upon me, all this time, I was still motivated.

Hearing other women screaming in excruciating pain, I couldn't, not even when I tried. I bit my lower lips instead and whipped my fingers. This continued every time the sharp pain came. I felt a mixture of things, it seemed like my heart was going to stop, I saw dark, I saw rainbow, the galaxy, man! The pain was truly intense.

A nurse observed my expressions and recognized I was in pain. She asked "are you alright?" Under regular circumstances I may have responded, do these expressions look alright? This experience however, called for humility so I responded very calmly, No I am not, I am in pain.

She quickly gathered my stuff and I was off to the delivery room. "Why did you bring Mrs. Tucker in here?" asked the same doctor who completed the procedure on me. She is ready. Oh no! He responded, it is has not been seven minutes since I was done with her. She cannot be it has not even been 15 minutes since I completed that procedure. I was assisted on the delivery bed, the entire team had a laugh, I came into the delivery room with everything neatly fixed and in check; despite my pains, underwear, half-slip[1], and nightgown were still being worn. Everything was in check. The doctor asked me in a jovial tone, "so Ms Tucker, how this baby passing out man?" I chuckled and got in line for my examination very briskly.

After checking he replied, oh yes! She sure is. He then told me, if I continue the way I started my baby will be there sooner than I can imagine. This aroused my excitement and the labor process intensified. Despite being in excruciating pain, I remained optimistic. However, my optimism was punctuated by the discussion of the medical team. I had no passage for normal delivery. I silently cried out, Lord have mercy!

The next moment was an emotional rollercoaster as the situation started to deteriorate. I started to panic baby Jenae was plunged into distress, she started losing oxygen. The gas mask stopped functioning as the oxygen in the cylinder finished while I was being transported. Both my life and that of my baby were in jeopardy Can anyone believe this? It was at this stage I realized motivation can be depleted, mine certainly was. As hope diminished I ask the Doctor in charge to send a message to my husband and mother, it went like this, "please tell

---

1 A half-slip is a piece of lingerie that is worn underneath skirts and dresses. It is also called a waist slip, or "underskirt", and is held on to the body around the waist by means of an elastic waistband.

my husband and mother who are standing outside, to take care of the baby."

The doctor paused the serious activities to yell, "Will you Shut up!" The last thing a pilot can do is tell the passengers they are about to crash. Listen to me, you are going to do this and you will succeed! At that point I do not know where the strength came from but the enemy was expelled from my presence. I saw life, prosperity, success and everything positive in the blink of an eye. Then like a breadth of fresh air, the cry of a bouncing baby girl broke the silence. Even in the distress of childbirth, having lost lots of blood, being torn physically and during excruciating pain, success was claimed by the doctor, who led the team.

As I reflected on the relics of that dreadful day, some distinct things from my ordeal remain etched in my memory. I recalled hearing my skin tear like the sound of cloth, although at that time, I felt no pain from that tear, I was more focused on delivering a healthy baby. When we focus on the negative things, they can impair the progress of positive and great things. I believed the words of the doctor. I did not stop to ask why he was yelling. Even though I do not like people shouting at me, I knew he sensed what was happening and had to use a strong method to keep me focused. Sometimes we focus on the wrong things when we are striving to achieve our goals. I focused on my goals and not the person who was placed there to help me. I felt I had reached my threshold and was about to give up for me this was the end of my journey. I felt my heart getting weaker, my body felt numb, all I saw was death. Thankfully, the doctor saw beyond what I saw, he was not on that shift by accident; he was divinely placed there, even the team of nurses were there for a reason.

One nurse bluntly told me, "you get pain after pleasure" She didn't know I was married, she even thought I was a teen. Regardless of her assumptions, those words were inappropriate and distasteful. The fact still remains that we live in a highly judgmental society. People will have many things to say given stereotypes and expectations positive and negative, however, we must choose what we allow to penetrate our psyche. We ought to be selective in choosing to information that strengthen and empower us. Another nurse said, "La-Toya look at me, keep your eye on me, listen to what I am telling you and she kept saying, you are strong, you will make it, you can do this", every time I looked at her, she smiled.

The moment she left to call for emergency assistance through the intercom, another panic wave rushed through my body. We must maintain composure and be able to understand who our dedicated cheerleader is. That person will lift us up when everyone else humiliates us. That person will always have a message of inspiration, hope and optimism. If you have not encountered your cheerleader/s as yet, no worries, one will come at the appropriate time.

Lesson Learnt

Some life decisions are best made when you make them for yourself.

Motivation Tip

When everyone says you cannot do "it", listen to your heart and chose to do or not to do based on your heart and not what others say. Consult with God and make agreement based on His guidance. Ensure that your agreement has a positive focus. Keep it positive and maintain your inner peace,

Chapter Six

"This Battle is not mine"

I vowed that I will not be in the delivery room again, after that bitter-sweet experience with Jenae. Mothers, wives and even husbands know what that means, many times the vow like many other vows are broken. So there I was, less than three (3) years later, masking the fear having realized that I was pregnant once again.

This time I concealed my pregnancy, not because of shame but it was my choice. One day my husband had to travel out of the town, so he asked me to purchase a one hundred pound bag of fertilizer and ask the driver of the car to take it in for me. He specifically told me, to pay the driver to take the bag in for me, to which I agreed.

The driver subsequently brought the bag of fertilizer from the store to the vehicle and we travelled home. When I got home, instead of the driver putting the fertilizer to my door, he left it at my gate, when I insisted he started to behave raucous and I was now left with a challenge. It was either for me to go inside and leave the fertilizer outside, with the possibility of someone stealing it, knowing that it was a farming area and a 100 pound bag of fertilizer was valuable. I stood waiting for someone to pass to request assistance. I stopped more than five persons who all indicated they cannot help. Some noted that it was too heavy; others said they cannot carry weight and the excuses continued. It started raining and I did not want my husband's fertilizer to get damaged.

I was therefore left with no other alternative than to drag the 100 pound fertilizer alone to the door of our home at being three months pregnant. When my husband came home and was apprised of what transpired, he was scared, upset at me and peeved at the rude driver. We subsequently visited the doctor and everything was fine. Sometimes we take some unnecessary risks that seem necessary for us. I learnt from this experience and made a personal commitment to make healthier choices, especially during my period of pregnancy.

I countered my fears with positive thoughts and feelings. My illnesses during the second pregnancy was worse than the first, this resulted in hospitalization twice. This did not demotivate me, as I was elated when I found out the baby was a boy.

Awesome news for daddy, who wanted his *'lickle bwoy'*, things were really looking up. We were ready to embrace our bundle of joy. However, an air of despondency replaced the joy and expectancy as due date passed. However, labour signs started; at twelve mid-night, on my impending clinic date. The journey had begun.

Upon arrival at the hospital, in excruciating pain, I was placed in a wheel chair, contrary to my first experience where I walked into the hospital. Upon examination, the nurses indicated I was dilating rapidly and was given an injection to soothe the pain.

The injection administered was called *Pethidine and I was not aware of the requirement* to remain in bed as a precautionary measure. As such, I independently took a bathroom break; it was on my way back that a sensation of hospital orbiting me around me took over.

Thank God for angels, a janitorial staff saw my actions and rescued me from falling. She alerted the medical staff who then advised me to stay in bed. Just as I reached the bed there was a gush of liquid flowing down my legs. It was a mixture of blood and some bodily fluids. The nurses were informed and I was quickly whisked off to the delivery room. The morning was still early as the place was still dark.

My phone went dead after I returned from the bathroom, so I was unable to inform my husband and mother that I was heading to the delivery room. I went into the delivery with the hope of being able to return in a few hours and have my phone charged. This was apparently only in my head, as the reality was totally different.

I breathed a sigh of relief; this journey was finally going to be over but was unaware of the precarious journey ahead. Pain intensified even as I prepared to deliver Jediel. I was fully dilated and set in the delivery position when it was discovered that the doctors and nurses were seeing his head. They instructed me to push. I pushed with all my might and with all that I had but there was no progress. The process continued the same way for several hours. My legs were tired and I was about to drop them when a nurse saw and assisted in holding them in position. She explained that I can kill my baby if my legs moved. It was after more than ten hours, the medical team concurred that Jediel was stuck. Nurses and doctors asked me to push, I did all I can and the nurses were convinced that I was "lazy" oh the pains women experience. The nurses I believe all had their own challenges, or were hardened from their experiences; I could not fathom nurses were as cruel as those who provided care.

They have said some of the most demeaning things to me that I have never heard before in my life. They laced me with negative remarks. "You are a good for nothing mother" "Not even push you are willing to push to save the baby". The comment that struck my heart was, "she will deliver a dead baby, and I personally want to sign the document and I will see to it that they jail her, because she is too wicked". My heart sank in a dark place. It seemed like all the energy I had was no longer available. Many times during my experience, I questioned if the ordeal was real, or if it was only a dream. It was a very sad reality. I called for help and no one came. There was one nurse who was seemingly kind, perhaps she was, but became frustrated and she too left. Even though I was in a room with others I was ALONE. I was alone entirely, I had little Jediel who was patiently waiting but above all, I had GOD. I vividly recalled praying loudly.

At this time, I appreciated being alone, I focused on God and what I was instructed to do by Him. The same nurse who wanted to sign the document said, "look the devil herself ah pray". Little did she know that God hears every prayer, the answers may not be what we want it to be. Nonetheless, He hears the prayer of the good and the bad. Not only did He hear my prayer but He answered it.

A doctor came into the room to get something, and realized I was in distress. She quickly came over to help, but realized I needed more help and time. Knowing that she was unable to do so at the moment she directed the nurses what to do, she explained she was going to do a surgery, so she could not help any further.

The doctor returned from the surgery and was expressing with the nurses how successful it was and how tired she was when she saw me in the same position. I clearly overheard her, "this is now an emergency, that baby will be an "invalid", "please go over and explain to her; the possible consequences of her actions of not trying to push". The doctor further shared; "please let her know based on how long the child has been there, there will be oxygen deprivation in the baby's brain". While the words were not her exact words, that was the essence of what was shared. The nurses came and the doctor came herself, she explained based on where the baby was, when they cut me, he may get cut too. Whether it was real or meant to scare me I said yes to everything. The nurses were asked to check the heartbeat of the baby. To their surprise Jediel's heartbeat was **NORMAL**. I was taken to the theatre with my legs elevated in the labour position to push. The rest was history and I was awakened and taken to the ward, where a bouncing, 8 plus Jediel was brought to me.

He has two dents on his forehead that are permanent scars to remind us of the ordeal.

Nevertheless, the important thing was, he was healthy, happy and handsome. Some speak poverty but God speaks prosperity over your lives. What do you speak over your life? This experience has proven that I can have success: even in distress. I lost lots of blood, I lost energy, I lost strength but I did not lose my trust in God. I gained encouragement by Him representing me yet another time in the labour process.

When asked, if I will have other children? With a smile my response is always, whatever God wants, He will direct. I know my God loves me and I am confident that He only gives me what He knows I can manage. Complaints against the nurses were being prepared, however, my family chose to pray instead. The power of prayer began to be manifested by the time my baby and I were ready to be discharged. Each nurse who comprised the delivery team came to check on us. They could not conceal the guilt, as some showed remorse by their actions, others from their tone. This was a powerful testimony of how prayer transformed their actions.

Lesson Learnt

God works in ways beyond our understanding. When we feel like giving up, it is often the times when we are about to get our blessing

Motivational Tip

Never give up when all others give up on you, always remember God has the final verdict, it is not done until He says, it is finished.

Chapter Seven

"Patience is truly a virtue"

*J*ediel was happy to be at school. He played and laughed with his teacher and things were going well. I left him feeling comfortable, knowing that he was happy, besides, he loved his teacher dearly. When my mother went to collect him later that afternoon, she was informed that he was not feeling well. She quickly called and informed me. I remember clearly saying to her "please keep me posted". Approximately two (2) hours later I received a call and immediately recognized the panic in her voice, all she said was "stop what you are doing and come home right now". I froze for a few seconds, managed to inform my supervisor that I had an emergency and I was on my way...

I have a principle where my family takes precedence over my job. Some may call me crazy but I can always get another job. Therefore, my family comes second in my life, after God. So I did not seek permission to leave but rather respectfully informed my supervisor. She sensed the urgency and allowed the organization's driver to take me home.

On my way home, I kept praying and I was exploring in my head what the call meant. I thought of several worse case scenarios.

Within fifteen (15 minutes) I was home and my heart plunged at the immediate sight. There was my mother sitting with a neighbour on our stairs, holding Jediel. I immediately rushed from the vehicle to find out what was wrong. She was numb, tearful and disoriented. After regaining her composure, she explained Jediel stretched out in her hands with his eyes rolling and was unresponsive.

I tried to remain calm and proceeded to research the signs and symptoms my mum shared. My research revealed the term "febrile convulsion".

I further consulted with a nurse who advised monitoring of his temperature. After being reassured it was nothing to worry about, I followed the precise instructions given by the nurse and monitored the improvements in my son's condition. He eventually slept and we relaxed. I was awakened in the middle of the night by a nudge from Jediel who requested some water. As I was about to get the water his request changed to tea. The tea making exercise was suddenly interrupted by the crashing sound behind me. Yes, you have guessed right, my toddler was on the ground with his body jerking uncontrollably. At this point he was unresponsive and the crashing sound brought the remainder of the household rushing to the kitchen. I immediately started praying loudly and a few minutes later we were in the vehicle heading to the hospital in our sleeping clothes. This was an emergency and any delay could have been devastating. Jediel regained consciousness on our way to the hospital but at this time his temperature was hot enough to fry an egg. We were attended to quite quickly and the nurses asked me to give him a bath. He cried profusely throughout the process, not because of the bath but he was hypersensitive to his privacy being exposed. Some of the nurses were rather emotionally illiterate. They found it strange to hear an 11month old having concerns with privacy. One of the attending nurses gave us a container for him to urinate so they can administer a urine text. I calmly told the nurse, he is not going to urinate in that container in front of you. She responded, "then if he ain't do it, we gun gah fuh tek it" She was insistent that he needs to urinate. She then used a catheter to insert into his tiny penis.

This was another experience where I felt helpless. Jediel cried uncontrollably until he was voiceless. When the medical team was finished, I perceived my son's confidence in me decreased. I had continuously assured him that I would protect him but this time I was unable to keep my word. For a brief moment I appreciated knowing the disconnect Jesus felt with His father when He cried out on the cross. While I am in no way able to be like God to truly understand that separation, my experience gave me a minute glimpse and it was not a pleasant one.

Just as I had researched, the doctor diagnosed febrile convulsion. I smiled within, though I was sad about all that transpired, because I was able to understand what was happening. Although, the doctor in no way tried to keep me calm, I had the peace of God within, reminding me that he will always be there. The doctors conversed and discussed my child's condition right in my presence and no one explained anything to me. I looked beyond that glitch because I knew what was happening even before going there but opted to remain humble and allowed them to do their job. At one point they were debating the possible cause. I interrupted the conversation by indicating, I do not have any medical record of epilepsy within my family neither does my husband's family. I further explained that Jediel had a fever as a result a cold, so the infection from the cold may have caused the fever, which resulted in the seizure.

I was rudely informed that they are the doctors and they know what they were doing. I again humbly accepted and patiently waited. After a series of tests, X-ray and examinations, he was admitted to the hospital for observation. Jediel refused to remain alone, so I stayed with him. Enveloped by chagrin and exasperation because no provision was made for a parent, hence, I stood for hours. At one point I stood with Jediel in my hand who refused to sleep on the bed. My neck back ached but the love for my son kept me strong. . Finally, a nurse saw my discomfort and offered me a chair. I sat on the chair and was able to get a few minutes sleep with him on my lap. Every time he went to sleep he jumped out with an indication like he wanted to cry. I knew my son was afraid, so I kept reassuring him that I will do all that I can to keep him safe.

I thought while I was experiencing this situation, how we often rely on other people when we have our challenges. Sometimes we rely on others who continue to hurt us, we rely on people who help with the intention of using it to their advantage and making us feel constantly obligated to them. Amidst all of this I could not help to think about the need to support each other. Instead of us depending on others we need to depend on God.

The doctor came the following day to inform me that the cold caused an infection that influenced the fever that resulted in the convulsion. I smiled because this was the exact diagnosis I shared with the previous batch of doctors I respect each professional and would not try to undermine nor do the work of others. This was a stark reminder that we often become territorial and haughty as professionals; however, being humble and open-minded are key tenets for success in our professions.

I was not ready for any confrontation, or any conflict, so I calmly listened, took all the guidance and our son was happily discharged. While his confidence in me decreased. I was happy to know he left understanding that Jesus still cares. Jediel is five years old today and he still believes Jesus cares for him and for all the other boys and and girls who encounter difficult situations. Moreover, the fusion of this experience and the many others I highlighted in this book, elevated my trust in God. The humiliation from insensitive professionals and the pain experienced were not sufficient to distract me from praising God. Jediel was subsequently discharged without complications. Despite the horrific experience with medical professionals during delivery in one country and another horrible experience in a different country, we still respect nurses and doctors and do understand that they are humans too. Sometimes they experience their own stress and challenges and are not able to compartmentalize and treat patients kindly. However, they are forever in our prayers and we will continue to trust and pray for them, that they will learn to exemplify kindness, humility and patience. Patience is important, especially during our trials as it critical to a successful outcome.

Lesson Learnt

Never harbour feelings of bitterness. Do not allow forgiveness to elude you. At times of deep pain, choose to forgive and live in peace.

Motivational Tip

Forgiving those who hurt you, helps you to heal from the hurt and pain, choose to forgive, heal and be restored.

Chapter Eight

Success amidst distress

*I*t was a bright sunny afternoon. As usual I called my husband Junior to check on him, he mentioned feeling sick. This was quite strange; I have never seen my husband sick for the years we have been together. My instinct suggested that I needed to worry but my husband recognized the change in my voice and reassured me, "I will be fine Latty". I felt a little better but was still concerned. I called a little later in the day and his condition didn't improve. I encouraged him to go to the doctor, he promised he would go. First thing the next morning I again pleaded with him to go to the doctor. He eventually obliged and I felt much better. The doctor gave him some medications and he returned home.

Three days passed and my husband indicated he was feeling better. However, when he developed a fever; I suggested returning to the doctor and explaining the new symptoms. He went to the doctor and he reminded me that he will be fine; besides, he is matured and can take care of his health. I believed him, mainly because we were miles away. The events to follow will be forever etched in my memory, I called and was informed, "Latty me deh at di hospital" I ran cold, my body froze, I was now in panic mode. He further stated that the nurses and doctors are around him and they are contemplating his admission. For a man who does not even get the common cold, more so fever and sickness for admission, you can imagine my level of anxiety at this time.

I was on my way to class when I received that news but could not focus for obvious reasons, so I left class early. I was discombobulated and really did not know what to do. I started looking for flights that same night and found none. I took the day from work the following day and I physically went to all the travel agencies and head offices of airlines in search of flights that Thursday and was told the earliest flight was Saturday.

I spoke with my husband the Friday morning and he indicated "the doctor is here, would you like to talk with him"? I responded in the affirmative. If I had only known what the doctor was going to tell me I may have said no. The doctor greeted me well. I identified myself and asked how Mr. Tucker was doing? The doctor's response shocked me out of my wits, my anxiety spiked and I was an emotional wreck. "Mrs. Tucker, your husband is in a serious condition, we received an almost dead man at this hospital". I could not fathom what the doctor said.

The few days seemed like eternity, the Friday when I spoke with the doctor, I wished it was Saturday. I was too weak to pray, so I cried. I could not eat nor sleep, there were so many questions. I eventually mustered some courage to pray. I was UPSET! FURIOUS! I pleaded with God, sought forgiveness for my doubt and tried composing myself for travel on Saturday.

Travelling to Jamaica or Guyana always brings a feeling of excitement. However, this time travelling to Jamaica was overshadowed by tension. There was no excitement. My reality struck when I arrived at the airport and my husband was not waiting for us as is customary. My children and I waited over an hour for a good friend of our family to pick us up from the airport. He explained not wanting to wait, so he delayed his arrival. His explanation knocked me like a bowling ball. My husband waits for us every time, because we are his and he is ours, (he is mine).

Right then my eyes were filled with tears but I tried to remain strong for our children. Instead of going to a hotel or the place to stay, we went directly to the hospital. I went to the nurses' station and was asked to wait in the waiting area. I waited excitedly to see my husband. However, the sight of him being brought to us in a wheel chair crushed me to pieces. I could not hold back the tears any longer. Even as I type these words, and it has been over two years, the image is still fresh.

Our son said "mommy I need daddy to walk again", I answered in my emotional state and reassured him that he would walk again. Our daughter said "will daddy be living in that white house all the time, where we cannot stay with Him?" I did not tell my children anything prior to our arrival, in an effort to be strong and keep them calm. After we left the hospital and went home, I explained everything to them, so for our next visits they were more informed.

I spoke with the doctor who explained that, when my husband arrived at the hospital, his kidney and lungs were dysfunctional and his stomach was closing in. My husband had a high tummy, swollen feet and arms. It was suspected leptospirosis. I was not a medical doctor but the diagnosis seemed off to me. That night I commenced an intense search for possible diseases based on my husband's signs and symptoms.

I arrived at the hospital every day before the nurses for the 7 am shift and left after the nurses on the night shift. After a few days Junior started to show improvement physically. Talk about the power of prayers! When I was finished with my research, I shared my findings with Junior. His words to me were, "you need to remember you are a Psychologist and not a medical doctor". Our conversation was interrupted when the doctor came for his daily visit. "I have some updates to provide Mr. Tucker". I was eager to hear the updates. He explained to my husband that the suspected diagnosis was inaccurate, after they realized his body was not responding to the treatment. He then turned to me and informed me that my husband would have to start dialysis since his kidney was not recovering. When he said this, I immediately said, "Doc, with all due respect, this will not be". He then asked if I was Christian, I responded in the affirmative. He said, "let us see, if it improves within the next two days, we can do a discharge with a referral for him to see a specialist".

My husband was given a time frame for his kidney to show improvement. The doctor indicated a specific number that should be read before it can be stated that improvement is seen. I was confident that his kidney will improve. The time came and the doctor returned with the blood tests and other results. I was already giving God praise before he announced the results. When the doctor indicated the improvements I said "My God is real!" I immediately stopped to offer a prayer of thanksgiving.

My husband was discharged, the bills were paid, medications received through the pharmacy at a separate cost, and God was still providing. Efforts were made to see the specialists but to no avail, since the specialist was in high demand. We went home and I was extremely happy to have my husband. I booked flights for everyone to return to Guyana. Both Junior and the doctor were a bit sceptical of this move. Some of our friends and family were also apprehensive, however, I reminded them that God does not change, the same God who healed him will protect him.

I took the leap of faith and we were about to leave the island without seeing a specialist. On our way to the airport, we stopped at the doctor Junior saw initially to provide him with an update. When the doctor read the blood tests and other results, you would not believe what was discovered. I tell you sometimes life has some unusual ways of revealing certain lessons, through specific experiences. Just as the Pandemic brought challenges and blessings, so do some experiences and situations.

The doctor recognized that Junior was bitten by something poisonous. The doctor expressed this, after the other contributors to the results he had been ruled out, leaving the poisonous bite as the number one contributor. To our surprise, Junior had a Eureka moment, he then remembered he was stung by a centipede, as it is commonly called in Jamaica, He shouted, "Oh yea! mi jus memba seh one forty leg did bite me fi true". There was no need for any specialist at this time, as the doctor D stated, "ensure to drink lots of water and eat healthy foods, you need to build up your immune system". When Jr. visited Dr. D, he was treated based on what Jr. stated. All three times he visited he was not very expressive and did not describe his true discomfort, so he was treated based on what he shared. With the doctor at the hospital he treated based on what he saw when Junior came in at a semi-helpless state.

I usually try to see the hope and lesson despite the gloom of the situation. My husband loves to work tirelessly. I would regularly tell him, there is the need to relax sometimes and take things a bit slowly but he insists. When he became sick, we experienced significant losses; his farm had a number of crop spoilage. This was not of importance to me, neither was it of importance to him. We were all prayerful and concentrated on his recovery. There are times when we have to learn some lessons the hard way. We sometimes learn best when we are on our back. Just as the pandemic would have taught some people what it means to relax, we need to learn from our experiences what it means to find time for the family. Unfortunately, some people have learnt this the hard way. You may have lost a loved one, possessions, an opportunity or something very valuable. Whatever, you may have lost; think about the situation and analyze it to see what you can learn from that experience. There is always something to learn. We may not often or always be willing to recognize and accept the lesson, but that does not mean there is not a lesson. Do not wait until you have lost someone or something to acknowledge the lesson. What lesson is there for you to learn from today? You are not reading this book by accident or mere coincidence, you are doing so for a purpose that only you and God know and will understand.

Lesson Learnt

God has never allowed a battle to come our way without His approval. Everything we go through trusting God He will deliver, just as he has always done, excellently!

Motivational Tip

You are not in that situation by accident, don't murmur, instead; focus on the positive and choose to learn while being bold and confident.

Chapter Nine

"Just when you thought it was over"

The year 2020 has brought its fair share of challenges. We were unable to meet as a family to enjoy our vacation. This was enough to trigger depression. Not only were we away from each other but we were uncertain about the duration of our separation. It is often said, just when you think it cannot get any worse, I went to the bank to do a transaction and realized that there was no money in my bank account. Upon investigating I was informed that there was an administrative glitch and my salaries will be sorted in the shortest possible time. It seems as they were speaking metaphorically for that shortest possible time saw me wait for over six months before I was paid. During the six months, my family needs remained the same and in some regards became more demanding. Anyone with growing children would tell you about the monthly food bill alone, not to mention the tuition fees of our children and all other necessary monthly expenses. That six months I have had to stand still and see the salvation of God. There was a particular friend of mine, who ensured that I received a consistent monthly pocket change. This was often done in some creative ways, my friend would put the envelope in places I visited regularly and there was always a motivational note attached. Every time I receive that change, I became emotional; this reminded me that angels still exist. We often expect to see angels with wings but there are angels around us whom we fail to acknowledge. God has provided in the least expected ways. Every money received came at the right time, every motivational thought shared came at a time when I was at my lowest and every grocery or kind deed shared came when we needed to as a family. One day our meter credit was about to end, I hadn't any money and did not know where any was coming from, we prayed and continued our activities until one of the children brought it to our attention that the meter had stopped beeping, to our surprise money was placed in the meter, after making several calls and everyone said no, we were reminded by one of the children again that we prayed asking God to provide maybe it was Him. We often ask God for things and ignore Him when the things are provided. We felt bad as adults but were grateful for the timely reminders through the children. When we pray we must do so believing, when we pray believing we will receive.

When I receive my salary, not only was I deprived of earning for six month but my monies were deducted without a reason. Efforts to query yielded no good result. There are times we are the recipient of unfair treatment, instead of looking to the persons who initiate it as the wrong doers, we often need to remind ourselves that they are mere instruments.

Instead of being upset with them, we should pray for them and say positive things about them. This seems impossible but you must remember that un-forgiveness is a terrible thing. Forgiveness keeps you looking young, fresh and relaxed. The experiences have reminded and in some instances taught me how to truly trust in God irrespective of the challenges.

During this period when all of this was happening I decided to continue serving God, a virtual program for children was initiated and the Gospel Ministry started with the children. The first challenge the

Ministry received was a negative response when we approached a reputable entity seeking permission to use their studio.

Even a virtual evangelistic campaign was organized where our children were preachers; this campaign reminded me that I am the Lord's anointed. The challenges were insurmountable, from videos being edited incorrectly, late nightly uploads, insufficient storage space on devices, power outages, no internet and the list goes on.

As if the challenges experienced were not enough, I became physically unwell and was unable to complete some basic tasks, I recovered and the work continued, only to realize my mother was unwell. She became unwell, and this bothered me emotionally, I worried endlessly about her being well. I started verbalizing my anger and frustration to God. Just while I was arguing and venting within my thoughts I heard a voice. I stopped to look around to see where the person was, having looked and realizing that no one was there I started listening closely, and I heard, "you will succeed, today you will get tasks done and please use this as a reminder that I am still here" I became weak and I felt ashamed. Over the years I have had similar experiences where I started venting and expressed frustration at God just seconds before a breakthrough. That particular day was truly successful for me. I got tasks done, received some good news and I was truly reminded that success can be achieved even amidst distress.

During the campaign, I was completing my quarterly studies and my two courses seemed like twenty-two. The demands were great. I told God if He allowed me to successfully complete my two courses and everything else that was happening I will continue to serve Him relentlessly. When the assignments came in quadruples, and time seemed limited I thought about what I told God. There were many times I felt like giving up.

I decided that I was unable to complete my studies and I reached out to my academic advisor. I was guided to reach out to my lecturer. After the conversation with the advisor, I prayed. I did not feel impressed to go through with the request to reach out to the lecturer. With much sacrifices and dedication, I was able to complete all my assignments. Not only was I able to complete all my assignments but I also achieved excellent grades, what more can I say than to God be the glory, great things he has done! I have decided to keep my promise; yes I will serve God relentlessly. I felt downtrodden, out of it and everything seemed lost, that was the time God came through for me. He reminded me that he has been the same yesterday, today and forever will be the same. I was able to prove yet another time that I can achieve success amidst distress.

During the moment of my confusion, part of what I experienced was a "bursar hold" on my account because my tuition was not yet paid. I was unable to register, view my grades, and access some features of my student portal. I was unable to view and confirm my courses for the upcoming quarter, unable to access my books and these frustrated me. Knowing that something similar happened and I had to sit out two quarters angered me. Every time matters as I was working fervently in completing my studies within a given time frame.

I was upset with God, while being upset I reflected on how consistent He was and I realized I need to trust Him. Instead of murmuring, I had to pause and thank Him. I remembered all the persons who inquired about access to scholarships. I remembered all the persons who were unable to continue their studies, I started realizing I needed to pray more and focus on all that God has done for me, and how He has been faithful along my academic journey. Just when I was wrapping up my reflections, I felt impressed to check my student page, only to realize the bursar hold had been removed. To God be the Glory. I immediately sent an email and by the next day, I received a call and was registered. While I had no idea about accessing my books, I am confident that my consistent God, already has this planned and my books and all other needs will be supplied. I continue to realize that I can achieve success amidst distress.

Lesson Learnt

Trust is not only saying I trust in God, it is also believing what we say and above all, believing in what God can do. I trust in God!

Motivational Tip

Trusting God is sometimes all we need, to see miracles happen. Trusting in God is letting go of all doubts, trust Him today, please obey and only Trust Him now!